THE AMERICAN COMPOSERS SERIES

T0051145

Samuel Barber: Ten Early Songs

(middle voice and piano)

ED-3859

First printing: July 1994

G. SCHIRMER, *Inc.*

DISTRIBUTED BY
HAL•LEONARD®
CORPORATION
7777 W. BLUEMOUND RD. P.O. BOX 13819 MILWAUKEE, WI 53213

TEN EARLY SONGS
(without opus numbers)

Samuel Barber said, "When I am writing music for words, then I immerse myself in these words, and I let the music flow out of this." In the songs of this collection (selected by John Browning and Thomas Hampson for their new recording on Deutsche Grammophon), Barber's flow of melody is endless. He had his reasons not to publish them; they do not always reveal the mastery of the later Barber, but they do contain many elements of the elegance and sophistication of the songs he did publish at this time ("Daisies," "Bessie Bobtail," Three Songs, Op. 10 [James Joyce], and "A Nun Takes the Veil"). The first two songs, "A Slumber Song of the Madonna" and "There's Nae Lark," are of particular interest. In fact, all of these songs, studied closely, give us an insight into the workings of the composer's mind, style, and personality, and in the crucible of this workshop we have an inkling of how he forged his mature style. As Browning and Hampson prove, they are expressive songs in their own right.

The subtle changing harmonic textures of "Slumber Song" are quite sophisticated for a boy of fifteen. And the adult emotional intensity of "There's Nae Lark," written two years later, adumbrates a constant theme of the majority of Barber's songs—the pleasures and pains of love. How did a composer so young come by such mature musical and emotional insights and have the ability to powerfully express them?

Besides being born with an innate gift, his social background can shed some light on his development. The artist who became Samuel Barber was, from the beginning, a darling of the gods. He was born into a genteel upper-class family where good manners, civility, and education were taken for granted. He was a precocious, highly intelligent, and perhaps an unduly introspective boy who was cradled in music from his earliest years. From the age of nine, when he announced he was destined to be a composer, his parents fostered this inclination. Born in 1910, he began serious study at fourteen at the Curtis Institute of Music in Philadelphia. Encased in an environment of culture, love, and security, Barber was denied nothing and given every advantage that money and taste could buy. But most important, and the central fact in his development, was his aunt, Louise Homer, a Metropolitan Opera star, and even more so, her husband Sidney Homer, an established composer of distinguished art songs.

Sidney Homer's songs were polished, refined, meticulous settings of literate poetry, never flamboyant. He belonged to the Boston School of American composers (which Michael Broyles has called "Music of the highest class") which included such fine musicians as George Chadwick, Edward MacDowell, and Mrs. H. H. A. Beach, among others. Homer encouraged, tutored, and advised Barber (who adored him) all his life. The nephew absorbed his uncle's style, aesthetic values, and judgments. One cannot overrate the influence of Sidney Homer—his serious craftsmanship and civilized taste left a deep imprint on the young Barber. It perhaps explains how Barber, during his formative years, escaped the often vulgar and mawkish parlor music (a mixed marriage of art song and popular music) that was the "rock" of it's day. Barber's family, like most proper American families, gathered round the piano and sang, but their songs were lieder and not the treacly sentiments of Ethelbert Nevin, Oley Speaks and company. This may seem to make the West Chester, Pennsylvania, Barber effete; in fact, the matrix of his growing-up years did have more in common with T. S. Eliot of Saint Louis, Missouri, than with Samuel Clemens of Hannibal, Missouri. But he was by all accounts, except for his intense musicality and emotional maturity, a serious but completely vital American teen-ager and worldly young man.

His songs were felicitous and well wrought from the beginning. They are not flashy and contain no bravura piano parts or cascading vocal lines. The introductions are terse and set the tone of the poem; the musical setting does not overwhelm the text; words and music have equal but separate functions; each explicates the other.

Barber was of Irish ancestry, so it is no wonder that many of his songs evince an Anglo-Saxon ambiance, although German romanticism (particularly that of Brahms) is not too far distant. The Gaelic influence is more evident in the later songs, except for its mild debut in "In the Dark Pinewood."

Yet in some indefinable way these songs have something American about them—perhaps because they are never rhetorical; emotions flair but they are kept within bounds; there is no Teutonic breast beating. The music and vocal lines progress naturally, almost effortlessly. And although Barber has not a note in common with the more rambunctious music of Charles Ives, he also in his elegant and refined way depicts and captures the world of an America we have lost.

There are cross references, idiomatic nuances, and stylistic benchmarks in the compositions of any composer. These songs of Barber are rife with such allusions. To cite a few examples: the momentum of their conservative, restless harmonic changes is characteristic of all of them. "There's Nae Lark" is a prime example of his Anglo-Saxon temperament. "Love at the Door" foreshadows the intensity of the characterization of Erica in *Vanessa*. Even more pronounced, the vocal line of "Serenader" strongly hints at *Antony and Cleopatra*. "Strings in the Earth and Air" has the deceptive simplicity of "Knoxville, Summer of 1915." "Night Wanderers" and the cynical "Beggar's Song" would not be out of place in the "Hermit Songs." "Of That So Sweet Imprisonment" suggests "Sleep Now." This game could be continued.

These songs, then, may not have been realized to the composer's satisfaction; he was abnormally self-critical. But they have the charm, graciousness, ardent rapture, and melancholy eloquence of all Barber's music. The effortless inborn sense of elegance, as in everything he wrote, is apparent here. The always controlled discipline of his technique never hid the heat of his turbulent emotions; his autobiographical music has always been the key to the man.

We should neither overrate nor underrate these songs. They show us the roads he traveled to become the consummate Samuel Barber. To any singer of art songs or any student interested in the evolution of American song, and those of Samuel Barber in particular, they are invaluable. All are stamped with his signature.

—PAUL WITTKE

These miscellaneous songs were discovered among Barber's manuscripts and are published here for the first time. They have been recorded on a Deutsche Grammophon CD (no. 435 867–2) entitled: *Complete Songs of Samuel Barber "Secrets of the Old."* The performers are Cheryl Studer, soprano, Thomas Hampson, baritone, and John Browning, piano.

The Collected Songs of Samuel Barber is also available for purchase in versions for high voice (no. 50328790) and low voice (no. 50328780).

A SLUMBER SONG OF THE MADONNA

Alfred Noyes

Samuel Barber
(1925)

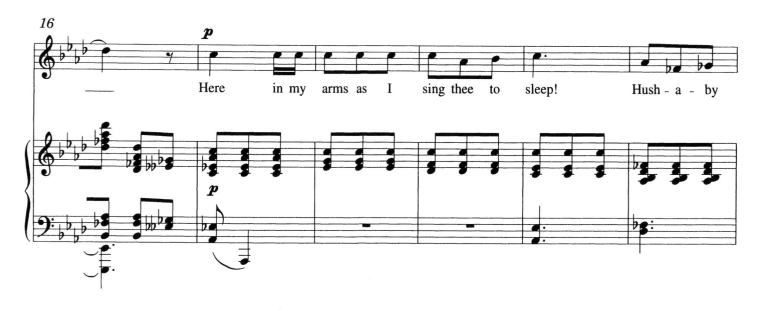

Here in my arms as I sing thee to sleep! Hush - a - by

Poco più mosso

low, Rock - a - by so. Kings may have won - der - ful

jew - els to bring! Moth - er has on - ly a kiss for her

THERE'S NAE LARK

Algernon Swinburne

Samuel Barber
(1927)

Two words were mistakenly printed in previous editions, corrected here:
* previously printed as "light;" ** previously printed as "hills."

Text used by permission.

LOVE AT THE DOOR

from the Greek *Meleager*
translated by John Addington Symonds

Samuel Barber
(1934)

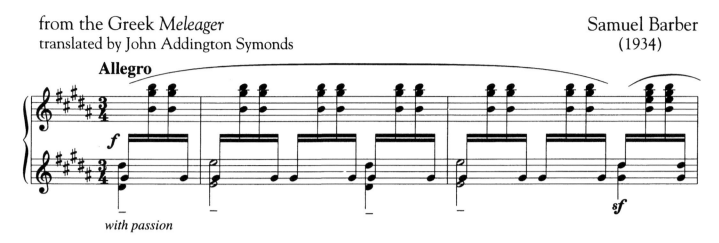

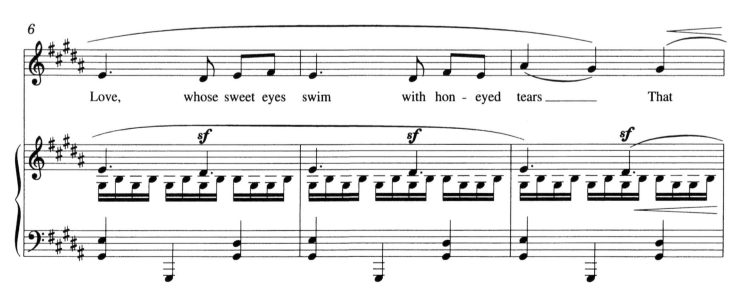

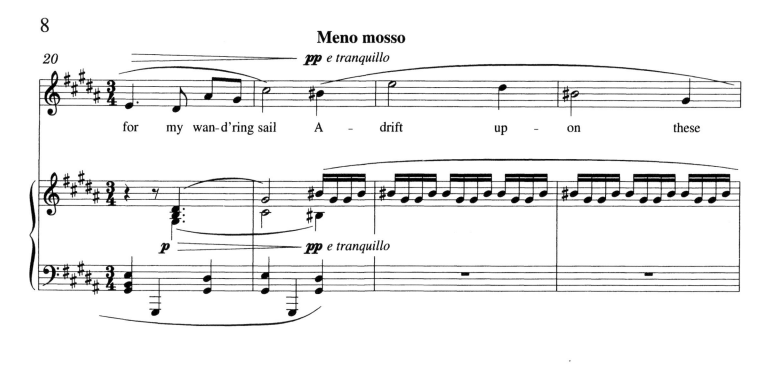

SERENADER

George Dillon

Samuel Barber
(1934)

Andante con moto

I have noth-ing that is mine sure To give you, I am born so poor What ev-er I have was giv-en

LOVE'S CAUTION

William Henry Davies

Samuel Barber
(1935)

Ran down the face of Heav - en this hap - py night. Her

Poco a poco più mosso

kis - ses are but love in flower, Un - til that great - er time When

gath - 'ring strength, those flowers take wing, _____ And Love can

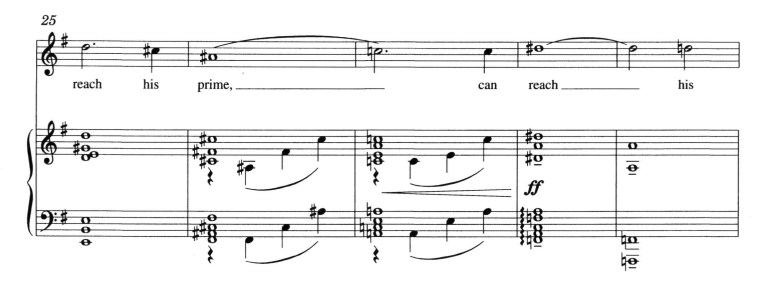

reach his prime, _____ can reach _____ his

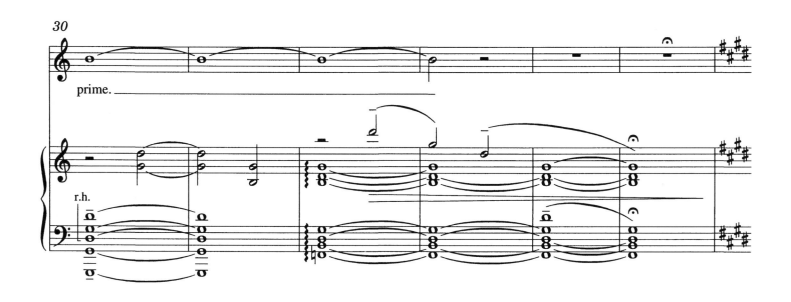

prime. _____

Tempo I

And now, and now, my heart's de - light, Good - night, good -

NIGHT WANDERERS

William Henry Davies

Samuel Barber
(1935)

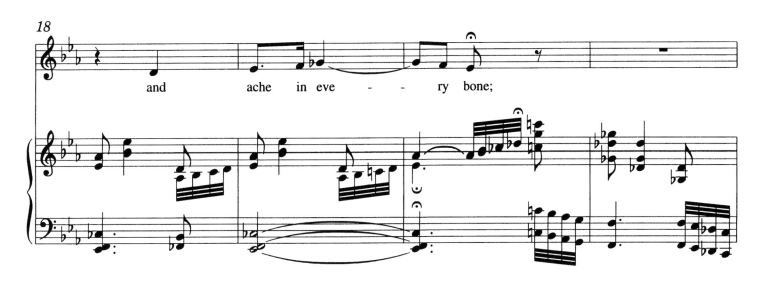

and ache in eve - - ry bone;

They hate _____ the night, they see no eyes Of

loved_ ones in ___ the star- lit skies. They see the cold, dark wa - - ter near;

30

They dare not take long looks for ____

33

____ fear they'll fall ____ like those poor ____ birds that see a

36

snake's eyes star - ing at their tree. Some of them laugh, ____ half

8va

OF THAT SO SWEET IMPRISONMENT

James Joyce

Samuel Barber
(1935)

Con moto

Of that so sweet im - pris - on - ment My soul,

dear - est, is fain— Soft arms that woo me to re - lent And

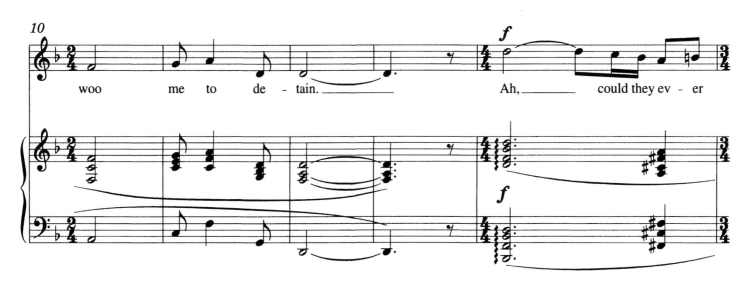

woo me to de - tain._____ Ah,_____ could they ev - er

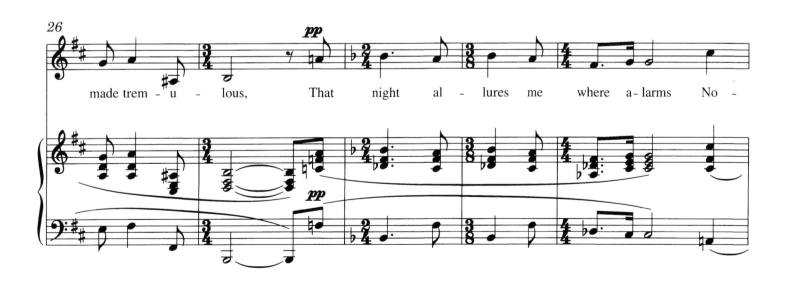

31

wise may __ trou - ble us; But sleep to __ dream - ier sleep be __ wed, But

35   *rit.*

sleep to __ dream - ier sleep be __ wed Where soul with soul lies

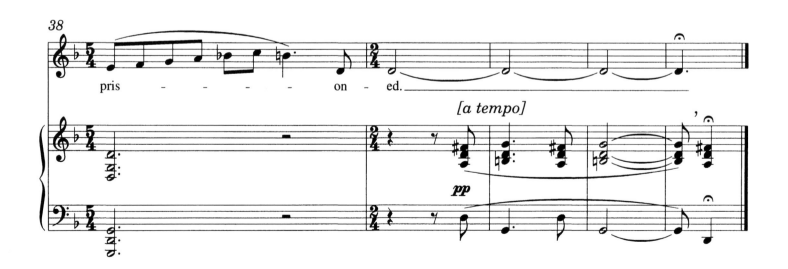

38

pris - - - on - ed. _____

[a tempo]

pp

James Joyce

Samuel Barber
(1935)

[Moderato]

Strings in the earth and air Make mu - - sic sweet;

Strings by the riv-er where The wil - lows meet. There's mu - sic a-long the riv - er, For

Love wan-ders there, Pale flow-ers on his man - tle, Dark leaves on his hair.

All soft - ly play - ing, With

rit.   *a tempo*

head to the mu - sic bent, And fin - gers stray - ing__ Up - on an

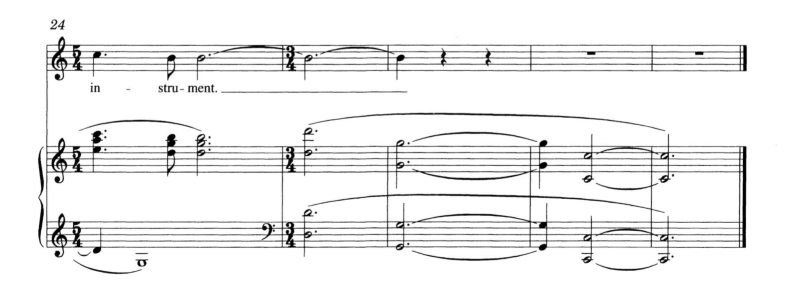

in - stru - ment.

BEGGAR'S SONG

William Henry Davies

Samuel Barber
(1936)

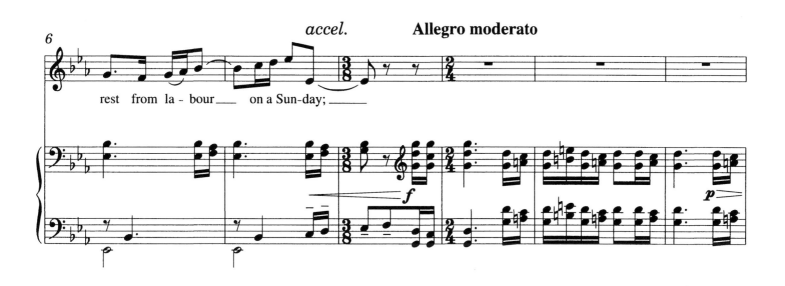

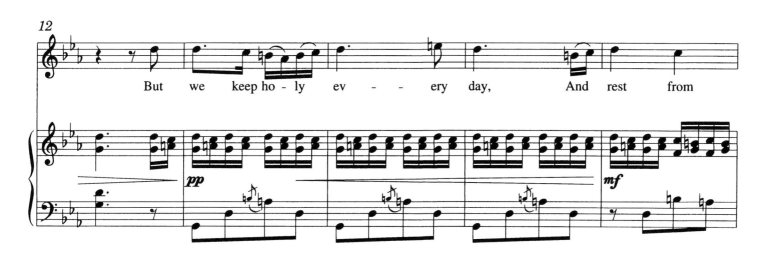

- - gars do _____ their part: _____ They _____ work, _____

cresc. poco a poco

dear la - - -

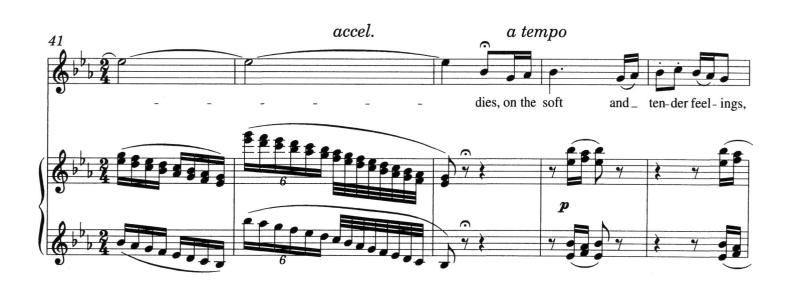

accel.   *a tempo*

- - - - - - dies, on the soft and _ ten- der feel- ings,

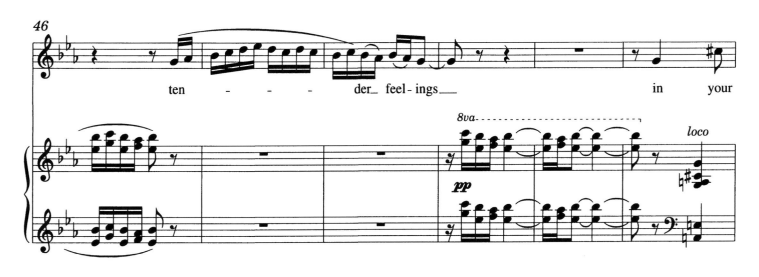

ten - - - der_ feel - ings__ in your

heart. _____

poco allarg.   *a tempo*

IN THE DARK PINEWOOD

James Joyce

Samuel Barber
(1937)